Two most common killers of seniors…

STRESS

AND

ROCKING CHAIRS

The "SAFE MONEY" Guide to Retirement

Author: **Chad C. Owen**

 INCREASEU

23 22 21 20 19 18   8 7 6 5 4 3 2 1

STRESS AND ROCKING CHAIRS–The Safe Money Guide to Retirement.
Copyright ©2018 Chad Owen

BISAC Category:
BUS050040 BUSINESS & ECONOMICS/Personal Finance/Retirement Planning
BUS027030 BUSINESS & ECONOMICS/Finance /Wealth Management
BUS036090 BUSINESS & ECONOMICS/Investments & Securities/Portfolio Management

Disclaimer: This publication is designed to provide accurate and authoritative information with regard to the subject matter covered. It is provided with the understanding that the author or publisher is not engaged in rendering legal or accounting services. If legal advice or other expert assistance is required, the services of a competent professional person should be sought.

Printed in Canada

Table of Contents

Introduction

After years of meeting with thousands of clients, sitting with people at their dining room tables who were supposed to be retiring, living the American dream, I have decided to write a book on some of the different cases I've run across. I have met with men in their mid-70s who now have to try and find a job because their retirement was blown up by Wall Street. I have seen older people break down in tears, wondering how something they had prepared for thirty or more years lost 50% of its value in a twelve-month period.

People like you and me—main street Americans—wonder if they will now outlive their retirement. On top of that, they now have to face people like the Bernie Madoffs of this world who they've trusted with their life savings that disappeared in an instant because the people they trusted spent their retirements on luxury homes, yachts, cars, and extreme lifestyles. I wonder how people like that can live their life of luxury while they are destroying the lives of so many people. Retirements ripped apart, grandkids now not being able to go to college or have a dream wedding. Greed is the root of corruption and dishonesty. These crooks remove themselves from any sense of morality by continually living a lifestyle that buries them in attention and financial fame.

I have said for many years, people who commit these types of financial crimes should be treated as murderers. I am sure there have been actual cases of seniors opening their financial statements and having a heart attack or stroke right then and there. There are other cases I have read about where someone found out what had happened to their retirement and savings and ended up killing themselves because they lost complete hope for their future and their loved ones' futures. You see, there are two common killers of seniors that few people talk about or realize. The two common killers are **Stress and Rocking Chairs**.

"Stress" kills because it causes all sorts of health issues that can lead to death. **"Rocking Chairs"** kill because retirees have nothing to live for or no money to do anything. One of the greatest causes of these two killers is retirements and savings being blown up by variable and risk money! Retirement money should **never** be put at risk. I will say that again: *retirement money should never be put at risk.*

In this book, I am going to address the many concerns retirees or those nearing retirement tend to have and explain the "Risk Money" and "Safe Money" options that are out there. I will also answer the many questions about the different products available, brokers, financial planners, marketing schemes, debt, and many other issues that retirees or those nearing retirement face. I hope you consider all the information in this book, apply it to your life and see how it's able to benefit you in your current financial situation.

No Longer the Days of "Father Knows Best"

I t was only in the last century we were told to get a good education, work for a good company, put money into our 401(k), and we'll be able to retire at 62 and live our golden years walking into the sunset of life. Many of you are in or are approaching your golden years, but due to misinformation and the greed of Wall Street, many of you do not have the gold. I have been in the retirement industry for quite a few years now, and most people I meet with did not expect it to be like this at this stage of their life.

Whether you are in your 40s or 80s, this is a blow to a lot of people's retirements. Part of the problem is we put our trust into the hands of other people to look after our retirements and never give it any thought because it was only numbers on a piece of paper. It's very easy to look at a financial statement or ignore it because you're scared to see what's in it. It's just as easy not to think much of it because numbers on paper don't seem to have real value. It's not until you retire when reality hits and you realize that everything you've saved has to last for the rest of your life. Then, you start to think about what you should have or should not have done to better prepare for this moment. The fact is, when we get caught up in everyday life, it's easy to put things that seem so far off on the back burner. What makes it worse is that we pay others to do this and trust that it's in good hands. One of the biggest misconceptions out there is that we have trusted government programs to carry us throughout our retirements.

SOCIAL SECURITY

Social Security was never meant to be security at all. Social security was enacted by President Roosevelt on August 14, 1935, to help limit the obstacles that come with modern

American life such as aging, poverty, unemployment, and to help widows and fatherless children. Social Security was never meant to fund everyone's retirement. Each decade there have been many, many amendments to the original Social Security Act. The amount of taxation has risen drastically, and the broadness of the coverage has expanded at such a rate that now Social Security is expected to be underfunded by trillions of dollars in the next decade or so. It is now a common belief of people in their 40s and 50s that Social Security will not be there when they retire. I meet with people all the time in their 60s to early 70s who believe the same thing.

Social Security is not and will not be enough for anyone to retire comfortably. It is common for Congress to give themselves a raise and not adjust the cost of living increase (COLI)[1] because they claim there was no inflation the year before. The Clinton administration greatly modified the way food and energy were calculated on the consumer price index (CPI),[2] which was and is a significant factor[3] in the cost

---

1 https://www.ssa.gov/oact/cola/colasummary.html
2 https://www.thebalance.com/consumer-price-index-cpi-index-definition-and-calculation-3305735
3 http://www.frontpagemag.com/fpm/91796/how-feds-hide-inflation-dick-morris

of living for those in retirement or on a fixed income. We all know as well that health care costs are rising faster than ever, year after year. With these factors in the COLI, Social Security payments will never keep up with true inflation and cost of living increases. As I stated before, Social Security was never meant to completely take care of your income during retirement.

401(K)S, 457, 403B, ETC.

These types of retirement opportunities were created to help people set money aside for retirement with tax deferral benefits and have only been around for the last forty years or so. Some of these plans allow employers to contribute to them. There are some major problems with these plans. Most of them have high fees and provide little help with your education on where and what to put the funds in. These plans usually have few options, and most of them put your retirement at risk due to market volatility. I have participated in these types of plans, and when I would call the 800 numbers for advice, I typically got someone who gave me vague answers and provided little to no help.

If you're in this type of plan, do not rely on your plan administrators to watch your money or to let you know when your accounts are losing. It's up to you to keep track of your money. I'm not sure why there are such high fees. Currently, there is talk of making the fees more up-front and known, but that is still in the legislative process. I am very tired of hidden fees and surprises. I cannot tell you how many calls I've received from people who haven't checked their statements and are shocked when they open them to find they've lost a significant amount of their retirement. I am not suggesting you stay away from these plans; just keep track of the movement of your money, whether up or down.

The good news is there is a bill going through Congress to make it mandatory to have a fixed annuity option in these types of retirements to protect you from market risk and provide full disclosure of all fees. Unfortunately, this process can take a long time and end up in years of legal battles.

PENSIONS

Pensions are the oldest of the bunch, dating back to the revolutionary war. Pensions are offered in many different ways and amounts in today's market. To make it easy to understand, pensions are simply defined as a way to continue paying a retired employee after they are no longer working. Once someone has retired, they can draw from the company's pension fund. When you are getting ready to retire, be sure to ask how well the pension is funded. The company should give you a percentage. You want to make sure they are adequately funded. Some pensions will allow you to take a lump sum instead of lifetime payments. If the pension is underfunded, the company could be experiencing financial problems, and you may want to take the lump sum and put it into a Safe Money account if possible.

Pensions usually allow you to take 100% or 75% lifetime with 25% for spousal continuation, or 50% lifetime and 50% spousal continuation. You should speak with your human resources representative to find out the details. Some pensions are pretty good. Unfortunately, some companies are no longer offering pension programs. I have a friend who is a pilot for a major airline company, and their pensions were completely taken away. That means, for years they had contributed to the pension fund. And the employees were counting on them for their retirement, but in an instant, they were gone. My friend informed me that one year they took a 36% pay cut to keep the pension funded and that didn't even work.

Unfortunately, many companies have done this. Now with states and cities potentially being able to declare bankruptcy, what's going to happen to all the pensions of the state and city workers who have been working for thirty or forty years and are counting on their pensions to be there for a secure retirement? Pensions are not a guaranteed source of retirement. Some states have a pension guarantee account, but it's usually only up to a certain amount per month. Check with your state to see if they have one and if they do, find out what the limits are. There are some Safe Money accounts you can put the lump sum payouts in that will guarantee payments for the rest of your life with no risk. We will cover those in a later chapter.

QUESTIONS TO ASK YOURSELF:

➤ What type of retirement fund do I have with my current company?

_____

_____

_____

➤ If it is a pension, how well is it funded?

_____

_____

_____

➤ Once I'm retired, should I roll over my retirement to a less expensive account?

_____

_____

➤ If I am over 59 ½ and I do not want to risk my money in a 401(k), have I taken advantage of moving my money to a Safe Money account by making an In-Service Withdrawal?

_____

_____

➤ Have I spoken with a Safe Money Mentor to ensure my retirement money has no risk and guarantees a lifetime of income?

_____

_____

The Health Benefits of SAFE Money

One of the major factors for people who are getting ready to retire or are in retirement is planning how long they will live. Brokers like to pick an age and base hypothetical returns (guesses) to come up with an estimated amount you will need. The problem is, you don't know how long you will live and neither do they. When you plan for retirement, you need to make sure it will last the rest of your life, no matter what. On top of that, if you have a spouse, you need to consider them as well. What if you want to leave money to your beneficiaries? You cannot base all of this on a guess. When you think of all of this, it can add a lot of stress to your life. Then, imagine you have all of that planned out, and the market drops thirty, forty, fifty percent – it can blow all of those plans in an instant. Putting your money into Safe Money accounts and guaranteed products that ensure a lifetime of income can remove the stress from that part of your life.

A recent study[4] from Duke University found a link between how a key stock index performed and how many heart attacks were treated at their North Carolina hospital shortly after the recession began in December 2007 through July 2009, when signs of recovery began. When you think about it, it's common sense. It is well known that stress can cause many health conditions. When we're stressed out, our heart races and we don't sleep well. According to the Mayo Clinic, stress can cause the following conditions:

> **On your body...** Headaches, back pain, chest pain, heart disease, heart palpitations, high blood pressure, decreased immunity, upset stomach, sleep problems.

---

4   http://www.journalnow.com/news/nation_world/study-links-recession-to-heart-attacks/article_cf210840-fe0a-5f6a-a827-9f065ebcfec7.html

On your thoughts and feelings... Anxiety, restlessness, worrying, irritability, depression, sadness, anger, feeling insecure, lack of focus, burnout, forgetfulness.

On your behavior... Overeating, undereating, angry outburst, drug and alcohol abuse, increased smoking, social withdrawal, crying spells, relational conflicts.

I am sure many of you reading this book have felt some of these symptoms when you stress about losing or outliving your retirement. As I said earlier, the effects of stress on the mind and body have been known for quite some time. I believe we're unaware of the health benefits that Safe Money can bring. How we protect our retirement and our lifetime of income can affect the way we spend our last years. A lifestyle without Safe Money can end up being spent living a "Stress and Rocking Chairs" lifestyle.

HOW LONG DO YOU THINK YOU WILL LIVE AND HOW LONG DOES YOUR MONEY NEED TO LAST?

People are living longer than ever now and need to make sure they do not outlive their income. Two things I have learned from my clients over the years:

1. You will get older faster than you thought you would.
2. You will live longer than you thought you would.

Some 61 percent of baby boomers say they fear outliving their money in retirement more than they fear death, according to a survey of 3,200 baby boomers by Allianz Life Insurance Company.[5]

*Assumes a person is in good health
Source: 2012 Individual Annuity Mortality Basic Table projected for mortality improvement from the base year 2013, American Academy of Actuaries

---

5   https://www.allianzlife.com/about/news-and-events/news-releases/
     Press-Release-June-17-2010

It is amazing how long people are living now and even more amazing how fast longevity is increasing. As you can tell from the chart above, the gap between males and females has closed, and now we have to consider something that has never been addressed before: married couples increasing each other's longevity by almost six years! It doesn't even mention if you are happily married or not!

This concern about outliving your income must be addressed if you plan to eliminate or reduce the "Stress and Rocking Chairs" aspect of your retirement. Only a few retirement products can alleviate these concerns. We will go over those a little later in the book.

QUESTIONS TO ASK YOURSELF:

➢ Do I get stressed about my retirement accounts when they are losing?

_____

_____

_____

➤ Do I lose sleep at night worrying about outliving my retirement?

_____

_____

_____

➤ Do I have mood swings when I get stressed about money? Here is a helpful hint to find out that answer: Ask my spouse or friends.

_____

_____

_____

➤ Have I spoken with a Safe Money Mentor to address these issues about protecting my money and lifetime of income?

_____

_____

_____

Brokers - Are They Working for Their Retirement or Yours?

D o you ever get the feeling like you're bleeding in the water and there are a bunch of sharks surrounding you? Many brokers are aggressive people. They will do almost anything to get your money, and some even pretend that they actually care about you. I do have to say, I've met a few reputable brokers that truly do care about their clients and do look out for their client's best interests. But they are few and far between. There is a reason they've made quite a few movies about the greed of Wall Street, and the harm brokers can cause people. Movies like *The Boiler Room*, *The Wolf of Wall Street*, *The Big Short*, and *Wall Street* shine the spotlight on the true character of a lot of brokers. I know a few former brokers, and they've admitted to me how driven by greed they are. It's all about the car you drive, Rolex watches, $10,000 high-end suits, $1,000 pairs of shoes and the lavish living accommodations. If brokers focused on your portfolio as they do on their materialistic lifestyle, you would be doing a lot better.

The fact is, few brokers actively manage your accounts. They go into their Monday morning meetings, find out which stocks and mutual funds pay them the highest fees and push them. Most accounts and trades are based on computer calculations and not one-on-one personal account management.

I'll give you an example of this. I was at a client's house, and she was telling me how great of a relationship she had with her broker. She had about $220,000 and was bragging about how much she meant to her broker. I asked her if I could prove to her that her broker didn't really know her that well and that her $220,000 was not that important to him. We called her broker on speaker phone. She stated her name and said she wanted to liquidate her accounts in order to move them to another company. We heard silence on the line, and he then said, "I thought you trusted me and we had a great relationship." She said she was tired of losing money and wanted to go through with it. He then said, "Who is this I am talking to?" She gave her name again, and we heard silence for a few seconds. He then said, "Oh my gosh! You gave me a heart attack. I thought you were someone else."

Even I was stunned at this comment. He admitted on the phone that she was not an important client and he did not even know of her. Needless to say, she moved the money right away to our Safe Money accounts.

The other problem I have with brokers is that they are paid their fees year after year, no matter if they are losing your money or not. They say they don't like annuities, but hear me when I say this: **YOU** ARE THEIR ANNUITY! As long as you keep your money with them, they make their fees off of you year after year as long as you live. That is not how it's supposed to be. You are supposed to have income guaranteed for your life, not them getting guaranteed income as long as you live.

I have a couple of examples to show how ridiculous it is that brokers make money even when you lose it. Imagine you are an electrical contractor and you bid for a job. In the process of doing your work, you make a mistake and burn down half of the building. Do you think you should still get paid for your work? Another example: Imagine you are a truck driver. You are taking a load from Denver to Dallas, and along the way, half of the load gets dumped out on the road. As you can imagine, when you get to Dallas, you would not get paid, and you would probably never get hired again. Why is it when brokers lose half of your money, they still receive their fees, and you keep them as your broker?

To add insult to injury, when you lose half of your retirement and you're drowning, instead of throwing you a Safe Money life preserver, they throw you more fees, adding weight to your retirement, sinking you even faster. Another way they get your money is using terms and statements like "portfolio rebalancing" and "I am diversifying your account by moving accounts around." Every time they move your funds, they can receive a fee or commission. Besides, the only time you need to diversify is if your money is at risk. Brokers also say that risk is "opportunity for growth."

If rebalancing and diversification were the keys to managing the risk in your accounts, we should all fly to Las Vegas and gamble in the casinos. You see, if you went to Las Vegas and played every slot machine or card table, rebalancing from one table to the next, diversifying your money across slot machines and card tables, you would be rich right? We all know that is not true. There's a reason why Las Vegas casinos bring in billions of dollars in revenue every year. Every slot machine and card table is designed to do one thing—take your money! Brokers and other people who sell risk accounts are very good at confusing you as well. They throw a 100–300 page prospectus at you for each of your funds and expect you to understand it through and through. I have spoken with many clients that have had variable accounts who admit they never read the literature because it is so confusing and intimidating. That is no way to feel secure and safe about your retirement.

You get the feeling like they think it's their money and not yours. The fact is, it's your money, not theirs. If you ever try to move money out of your accounts to another company, you will find this out quickly. If you call the 800 number, they transfer you to your broker, and after you still decide to move your money, they have the Conservation Department call you to make sure you are making the right decision. I went to the bank once to pull out a large sum of money, and before I knew it, I was called back to the bank president's desk. When I sat down, he asked if I was sure I wanted to pull out that much money and that they could find a good place for me to invest it. I told him *no thank you* and said I still wanted to get my money out. I was then introduced to an investment advisor. At that point, I had to get stern, inform them that I was using the money to buy something and to just give me my money. I was blown away. It's my money, not the bank's! Many people feel like this regarding the people who manage their money.

To prove all my above points, I want to ask you one question: Why didn't they move your money when the market was dropping? This could have occurred for two reasons. One is they were not paying attention to your account. The other is they did not want to stop making their high fees and move you into the safety of a money market account or cash equivalent because most of the time, as soon as they move your money out of the risk accounts, brokers do not make as high of fees. Maybe it's time to fire the brokers and money managers that risk your money.

On a side note, be careful about getting too close to the people who manage or help you with your money. If you end up feeling loyal to them or that they are your friend, it can cloud your decision to move your money when it's time or when they lose you money. This is not about a personal relationship, it's about what is best for your retirement and having income you can never outlive.

QUESTIONS TO ASK YOURSELF:

➢ What has my broker done to help my retirement grow over the last ten or fifteen years?

_____

_____

_____

➢ Are they good about getting me out of the market when it's dropping and getting me into Safe Money?

_____

_____

_____

➢ Do they continually move my money around to make more fees and commissions?

_____

_____

_____

➢ Do they use phrases like "portfolio rebalancing," "diversification," or risk is an "opportunity for growth"?

_____

_____

_____

➢ Are they fee-based only and get paid even when I am losing money?

_____

_____

What Do Financial Planners Really Know?

W hat do all those fancy acronyms after money managers' and financial planners' names really mean? Most of the time, nothing. When I worked in corporate America, I had all sorts of people working for me that claimed to have these titles and degrees, yet they were still at an entry-level position. I even had people with degrees from Harvard and Princeton working at those entry-level positions. To me, a title means very little. You can get an online title or degree for just about anything nowadays. It's not someone's title that matters; it's what you've accomplished with it, how successful you've been and how successful you still are that actually matters. That's another issue, people who rely on how great they were and not how great they are.

If you want someone helping you with your life savings and retirement accounts, you need to have proof of how successful they are right now and what kind of continuing education they are taking to keep up with future changes in the retirement industry.

According to a Market Watch article from the *Wall Street Journal* on May 13, 1999, 85% of fund managers cannot beat the indexes. Even in 1999 when the market was booming, they still couldn't beat the indexes with all their so-called insight, titles, and wisdom. Nothing has changed in 2017. Only 1 in 20 fund managers actually beat index funds.[6]

Did you catch that? You have been paying 1 – 5% in fees for someone to manage your money when 85% of them can't beat the indexes. It kind of makes you angry, doesn't it? It's like you are throwing away your money to fees and missing more growth from the indexes. I can't even imagine how bad

6   https://www.marketwatch.com/story/why-way-fewer-actively-managed-funds-beat-the-sp-than-we-thought-2017-04-24

those numbers are now with the volatility of the market over the last couple of decades!

Here's another point I am sure you're not aware of. According to an article from *Investment News* on October 25, 2009, Morningstar found that 51% of the 4,383 funds it has tracked for manager ownership level over the last five years, fund managers owned no stake at all. The title of that article is *"Most portfolio managers shun their own funds."*

I was watching a major financial channel on television where a woman was a guest on the show, and she was recommending buying certain stocks. Every time she would recommend a stock, a disclaimer would appear onscreen stating if she or any of her family or friends owned the stock. The outrageous thing about this is, out of the six stocks she claimed were so great, one out of the six she had a little of and none of her friends and family owned. I am tired of financial professionals recommending products that they themselves do not have, nor do their friends and family have. It is all too typical though. They are so willing to risk your money but not theirs. There are quite a few financial advisors, money managers, and brokers that are always on the brink of financial ruin. Why is it that every time the market crashes you hear of some money manager or broker committing suicide? It is a high-stress industry that ties their identity to the materialistic things they own, which they can afford because of the high fees that come from you.

There's an alluring draw to financial planners and brokers; it's like a bug going into the light about to get zapped. All the fancy suits, high-end cars, and big expensive office buildings should **mean** nothing to you because all of that certainly **does** nothing for you. It's okay to have money, but it is not okay for money to have you! Most of them are highly driven by money and what it can get for them and not what it can do for you.

QUESTIONS TO ASK YOURSELF:

➢ What do all those acronyms and titles do for my retirement?

_____

_____

_____

➢ What funds does my money manager/financial planner have that they are recommending to me? Do I have proof that what they are saying is true?

_____

_____

_____

➢ Does my financial planner/advisor only deal with safe money?

_____

_____

_____

➢ Will this advisor give me all their current and past client track records of the gains and losses they have averaged for them?

_____

_____

_____

Wouldn't It Be Great If...

O ver my years of helping thousands of clients prepare for retirement, I've been told so many crazy, unrealistic, over-the-top statements that they've heard from brokers, bankers, financial planners, and other so-called money gurus. What if they had to tell the truth? What would their statements sound like? Here are a few of the statements they would have to make.

WOULDN'T IT BE GREAT IF YOUR BROKER, FINANCIAL PLANNER, BANKER SAID WHAT THEY MEANT?

- You pay me even when I lose you money.
  - o Who else can say they get paid when they don't do their job?

33

- I can offer you no guarantees of any kind!
- I really have no clue which direction the market is going – neither does anyone else.
- I am encouraged by my broker/dealer to push certain products even if they may not be in your best interest.
- When I disparage FIAs, it is usually out of ignorance or disregard for your financial objectives, because I really have no idea what you're talking about.
- I will tell you pretty much anything to keep your money with me.
- When I say, "The loss you've had is only a paper loss," I really have no idea if that is true.
  o If you need the money after a loss – IT'S A REAL LOSS.
- As far as I'm concerned, your money should ALWAYS be in the market and ALWAYS be exposed to risk, regardless of contrary financial indicators, thereby earning me the highest fees.
- You really should have the majority of your retirement money in FIAs because they are the only product that provides safety, security, growth without market risk and guaranteed lifetime income.

- I tend to forget that your money is YOUR MONEY. After a period of time, I consider it **MY** money to do with as I please. **YOU** are **MY** annuity that guarantees me **MY** income for as long as you live.

The fact is if investing your funds was such a great idea instead of putting your retirement accounts in Safe Money products, why are there so many retirees struggling to be able to retire with the money that was put into their company-sponsored plans? Safe Money accounts are the only products you should have when you are trying to plan for a retirement that will provide a lifetime of guarantees. Only Safe Money products provide the following four things:

1. Safety
2. Security
3. Guaranteed income you will never outlive
4. No market risk

It is critical to a successful retirement not to listen to hopes, dreams, what if's, or any other hypothetical language from "financial advisors." You want someone to provide guarantees to eliminate the financial side of dying from Stress and Rocking Chairs.

QUESTIONS TO ASK YOURSELF:

- ➤ Can my financial planner/advisor really predict what is going to happen in the stock market?

  _____

  _____

  _____

- ➤ Has my financial planner/advisor made stock, bond, mutual fund, or commodity recommendations in the past that have hurt my accounts?

  _____

  _____

- ➤ Have they made comments about losing my money as only a paper loss?

  _____

  _____

- ➤ Do they still make fees off me even when I am losing money?

  _____

  _____

All This Marketing...
Who or What Do I Believe?

E very time I turn on the radio, TV, look at a magazine
or open a newspaper, I see advertisements for buying
stocks, gold, silver, mutual funds, or some other get-
rich-quick scheme. People are telling you to take equity
out of your home and invest it or convert your IRA to a
Roth IRA. You hear terms like "infinite banking,""bank
on yourself," or how to retire tax-free using a life insurance
policy. I heard a radio commercial the other day about buying
gold and how they thought it was going to go over $5,000 per
ounce. I'm sure you've heard how to get 20% returns on your

investment money and how to guarantee a secure retirement as a millionaire. When all of this is in your face every day, it's hard to decipher which ones will work and what to believe.

The problem with this type of marketing is everyone who does this says their way is the best for you and it works for all situations and circumstances. A lot of these marketing ploys are just a way to get your money—and they want all of it. The fact is that some of these products work very well for you and are legitimate. No one product will work for everybody though. There have been quite a few instances I've sat at a table with someone or received a phone call and had to tell the prospect I would not be the best person to help them or the products I carry are not suitable for them. Let me give you an example of some of the product advertising you will hear on the radio, TV, newspaper or direct mail.

COMMODITIES

According to Wikipedia:

Commodities are basic resources and agricultural products such as iron ore, crude oil, coal, ethanol, salt, sugar, coffee beans, soybeans, aluminum, copper, rice, wheat, gold, silver, palladium, and platinum. Soft commodities are goods that are grown, while hard commodities are the ones that are extracted through mining.

"There is another important class of energy commodities which includes electricity, gas, coal, and oil. Electricity has the particular characteristic that is either impossible or uneconomical to store; hence, electricity must be consumed as soon as it is produced."

The problem with commodities is that they are all variable and you can lose money in them. A lot of the time, these commodities are tied to market demand, the economy, or are let out in controlled amounts for consumer use. I used to work in the diamond business, and I was under the impression that diamonds were so rare and worth so much. After a little research, I found out that there are stockpiles of diamonds and only a few at a time are released in order to keep the price high. We see this every day with oil and natural gas. This is definitely not something that is guaranteed to gain and should not be used as a Safe Money vehicle for your retirement money.

CONSUMER CONFIDENCE

This is pitched all the time through the media. They will say "stock market rallies on *consumer confidence.*" I have met with hundreds and hundreds of clients over the past market crisis and still, to this day, I have not met anyone with this so-called consumer confidence! Most of the people I meet with are still very scared of losing money and do not like the financial direction our country is headed.

THE MEDIA...WHOSE SIDE ARE THEY ON?

The people who cause these market frenzies are the media. Whether it's a newspaper headline, a news show on TV or some magazine promoting their own agenda, all media and its content stirs up some marketing opportunity or scheme for someone. The media feeds off of fear as do many salespeople. For example, when gas goes up to $5 a gallon, people start telling you to buy oil and the oil companies then say to raise the price of gas. Another example is the media will say that the dollar is crashing, so the gold salespeople say *hurry and buy gold, it's going up to $3,000 per ounce!*

I remember listening to a guy yelling on a major primetime show from a large news channel on March 11, 2008, telling you not to sell Bear Stearns, that it's fine and you'd be silly to get out! Six days later, Bear Sterns collapsed, and its stock went down 90%. As we know now, Bear Stearns is no longer around. There are numerous accounts of the media telling us one thing about the safety and security of the market and the next day, they'll be talking doom and gloom! What a crazy source of information and double talk.

QUESTIONS TO ASK YOURSELF:

➤ Where am I getting my financial information from?

_____

_____

_____

➤ What is their motivation to promote their products?

_____

_____

_____

Risk Money

R isk money is simply defined as any product you put your money in that could lose value. These products include stocks, bonds, mutual funds, REITs, 401(k) s, variable annuities, commodities, and many others. The positive side to risk money is you could gain a lot of money quickly. The downside is you could lose a lot of money just as quickly. Risk money is not a way to protect your retirement accounts. Risk money is typically associated with high fees. I'm going to share with you a few thoughts I have about risk money and those who sell it.

STRESS AND ROCKING CHAIRS

THE YO-YO RETIREMENT

If you've kept an eye on the market, you probably witnessed three very high highs and two very low lows over the past two decades. This pattern makes the possibility of timing your retirement challenging and inconsistent. I call this the Yo-Yo retirement. The market goes up, the market goes down, and the cycle repeats. I will give you a little illustration of why this type of investing is so bad for you. If you have $100,000 in your retirement and your investment goes down 50% and back up 50%, how much do you have? Back to an even $100,000? Wrong. You only have $75,000. What if it's reversed? You have $100,000, the market goes up 50% and then goes down 50%, how much do you have then? An even $100,000? Wrong again. You would have $75,000. Do the math, it's true.

$100,000	$100,000
-50% equals	+50% equals
$50,000	$150,00
+50% equals	-50% equals
$75,000	$75,000

As you can see, this kind of retirement planning or investing never works. Besides, think about what happened in March of 2009. If the DOW was at a 25-year low, then if you had $100,000 25 years ago, you would then have $100,000 25 years later. And that doesn't account for all the fees you had to pay and how much inflation has risen in that 25-year period. This is not the way to safety and security; this will take you directly to a life of Stress and Rocking Chairs.

LET IT RIDE

Another thing you might hear your broker or risk money manager say is "Let It Ride." The only other time I've heard this type of language is when you are gambling. People think all I have to do is pull the slot machine one more time and I will win big. I used to live in Las Vegas, Nevada and I quickly learned the consequences and fear gambling brings. I was married at the age of nineteen, and we had moved to Las Vegas. It was mesmerizing, all the lights and sounds of people winning money.

I took a roll of quarters and started playing the one-armed bandits. Ten dollars was a lot of money to me then! I quickly lost that money and began to panic. I went to my brother and asked to borrow a roll of quarters. I quickly lost that one as well. I started sweating, and my heart began to race. I went to my dad and asked for a roll of quarters. I had to recover the money I lost and started thinking how I was going to tell my wife that I had lost this much money! I went through that roll of quarters just as fast.

I had two quarters left. I felt defeated and devastated. I put the last two quarters in, closed my eyes and pulled the slot machine arm. I heard the machine go off; I won exactly thirty dollars! I cashed out my money, paid my dad back, paid my brother back and never gambled again!

Brokers are a lot like slot machines. When a slot machine pays out, it makes a lot of noise, clank, clank, clank, as the sounds of the heavy coins hit the metal trays. The funny thing is, when the slot machine is taking your money, you don't hear a thing! Kind of like your broker, when they're making you a lot of money they're yelling at you, look at all of the money I made you; look at how great I am. When they're losing your money, you never hear from them or can't get in touch with them. Do not gamble your retirement!

PAPER LOSS

If you've used brokers or risk money managers, I am sure you've heard this line. When you are losing money, they say, "Don't worry, it is only a paper loss." When you are making money, do you ever hear them say, "Don't worry, it's only a paper gain?" No, of course not, they just say how well they've done for you. The fact is if it's a paper loss and a paper gain, that makes a paper nothing. The other thing is, it's not a paper loss if you need to start drawing for retirement at that time. Quite frankly, I think "It's only a paper loss" is a very insensitive thing to say to someone who just lost 50% of their retirement. Would you allow your broker or financial advisor to risk your money if it wasn't on paper but a pile of cash right in front of you? Of course not!

After reading this chapter, you should understand that putting any retirement money into anything that has an opportunity to lose is not the best decision.

QUESTIONS TO ASK YOURSELF:

➢ Does the Yo-Yo retirement concept work for me?

_____

_____

_____

➢ Do I really want to gamble with my retirement?

_____

_____

_____

➢ Is it really a paper loss or an actual loss when I go to draw money out for my retirement in a down market?

_____

_____

_____

Safe Money

S afe Money refers to any type of funds you put your money into that has no risk of principal loss or loss due to market volatility. These types of funds are Certificates of Deposit, Fixed Annuities, Fixed Indexed Annuities, most Money Market accounts, and Cash. The whole purpose of Safe Money is to protect it and make sure you cannot lose. These are the types of funds you would make sure your retirement, emergency money, and savings are in. Too many times, we allow all of our money to be at risk. In today's market, there are a lot of products that provide safety and security, allowing you to participate in some market gains without any market

STRESS AND ROCKING CHAIRS

risk. I will give you some examples of how these products work and why they benefit you and your retirement.

It is extremely important to protect yourself from market loss. If you applied this concept to your retirement, you would never have to worry about market loss to your retirement and Safe Money. I know it seems like common sense, but you would not believe how many people I talk to every day who think they must get all the gains of the market to make their retirement work.

GONE FISHING

Allowing your money to be at risk is like being on a fishing boat in a stormy sea. Imagine, as you ride up to the top of the waves, you're allowed to catch a lot of fish, but once you're at the top heading back down, you have to dump out half of your load. Then as you head back up the wave, you're able to get back half of the fish you had to dump out. If you continued this cycle a few more waves, you would keep losing fish and going backward. Now, let's put you in another boat. As this boat rides up the wave, it's able to catch fish but not as much as the first boat. The difference in this boat though is on the way down, you're allowed to keep all your fish and maybe add a few more. If you continued to be in this boat, you would far out-fish the first boat. It makes more sense to be in the boat that never loses fish.

ELEVATOR

Another example of Safe Money is like having your retirement account on an elevator that only goes up. When the market goes up, the elevator goes up, but when the elevator starts to go down, you're able to get off on that floor and protect your money. Once it starts to go back up, you're able to start back where you left off. It's a win-win situation.

Safe Money is the only way to keep your money safe and protect your retirement. It's one of the best ways to keep you out of Stress and Rocking Chairs and allow you to sleep at night, not having to wake up in the morning worrying if your retirement is going to be lost in risk money.

QUESTIONS TO ASK YOURSELF:

➤ Do I have my retirement and savings in Safe Money?

_____

_____

_____

➤ Do I want to not worry about losing my retirement money?

_____

_____

_____

➤ Am I tired of all the ups and downs of the market?

_____

_____

_____

➤ Is it worth all the stress and constant worry about my retirement money not being there when I need it?

_____

_____

_____

INcome vs. IFcome

(Income Riders)

This is probably the most important part of retirement. It's not necessarily the amount of money you have, it's the amount of income you can get off of it for the rest of your life.

In a conversation with a client, we were talking about the amount of retirement income he could get when he retired in the next ten years. He pulled out an Excel spreadsheet that his broker put together for him and said he could get this amount of income in ten years according to his broker. I was in shock at the numbers the broker had told him; it was way too high!

I asked if I could take a closer look at the spreadsheet with all of the broker's calculations. It made me sick what I saw. The broker had run a best, middle and worst-case scenario for this guy. According to this broker, the worst-case scenario was an 8% return, the middle case scenario was a 16% return, and the best-case scenario was a 24% return over the next ten years.

I don't know what this broker was thinking! None of those figures were even remotely guaranteed or even close to reality for a ten-year period. He was giving this guy such a false sense of hope and security, it was not even funny! Unfortunately, this is not the first time I have seen this and I know it will not be the last. This was the truest form of IFcome. Only IF the market had that kind of return and IF the broker was telling the truth, would he be able to draw out that kind of income.

I only deal with products that have true INcome interest guarantees and provide a true INcome that you can live on for the rest of your life. There are plenty of products that will provide INcome, not IFcome.

HOW DO I GET GUARANTEED INCOME?

One of the most effective ways to guarantee INcome is to buy a Fixed Indexed Annuity[7] with an Income Rider, commonly referred to as a Hybrid Annuity. An income rider has a set percentage of growth with either simple or compounded interest for a set period of time or until income for life is started. It is very important to ask if it is simple or compounded interest. No matter what it is, don't get caught up in that. It's easy for someone to get caught up in a larger compounded interest and still end up getting paid less per month because of other factors such as initial bonus, payout percentage, etc.

Any good agent will have a comparison tool that places each insurance company side by side to show which company pays the most per month and per year. Remember, how they get to the income amount is not as important as the end result, which pays the MOST income for you. Insurance companies and agents can be pretty slick on how they come up with the income instead of how much the end number will be.

When your biggest concern is income for life, the only number that matters is which one pays the most. I know I

---

7   https://www.investopedia.com/terms/f/fixedannuity.asp

have repeated this a few times, but there's a reason why I have done this—I am trying to keep you from being misled.

QUESTIONS TO ASK YOURSELF:

➤ Do you want IFcome or INcome and what are the guarantees?

_____

_____

_____

➤ Has my broker shown me a worst-case scenario where the market has lost 50% in six months like it did in 2008 and 2009?

_____

_____

_____

➤ Is guaranteed income for life the most important thing to me?

_____

_____

The Dreaded Annuity
(How Do They Really Work?)

T he word annuity[8] used to be a bad word to many people, but not anymore. It still amazes me how this has happened. Annuities have been around since before Christ and were used as payments for Roman soldiers when they retired from service. The fact is, there are four core types of annuities.

Three out of the four are the safest types of retirement accounts available in the financial industry today. The four main types of annuities are Single Premium Immediate

8   https://www.investopedia.com/ask/answers/12/what-is-an-annuity.asp

Annuity (SPIA), Fixed Annuity, Variable Annuity, and Fixed Indexed Annuity. One of these is a wolf in sheep's clothing and is a major reason why annuities have received some bad representation. These annuities and financial products have been misrepresented by salespeople.It is very important to get all of the details and make sure your agent knows about all of the different options that are available. I will explain each type of annuity in detail in this chapter.

THE SINGLE PREMIUM IMMEDIATE ANNUITY (SPIA)

This is the easiest type of annuity to explain. You simply give a lump sum of money and receive a guaranteed payment based on your age, gender or the length of time you want payments. You can pick any length of time from one year up to a lifetime. The insurance company takes the amount of money, the time frame you want to receive payments and, if it's not a lifetime payment, they figure out how much you'll receive based on their calculations. If it is a payment for the rest of your life, the insurance company will take into consideration your age and gender. I am not a big fan of these because you give all control of your money to the insurance company.

THE FIXED ANNUITY (SLOW AND STEADY)

The fixed annuity[9] is a contract between you and the insurance company to guarantee a particular interest rate for a given period of time. These typically range from three years to ten years. These products are great to lock in an interest rate. These products do have restrictions, such as limits on how much you can take out and surrender fees for the length of the contracts. The interest rates range from 2% to 4% or a little higher depending on market situations and what the insurance companies are offering at the time.

THE VARIABLE ANNUITY (A WOLF IN SHEEP'S CLOTHING)

To me, this type of annuity is one of the primary reasons why annuities, in general, have received a bad rap. They are presented as safety and security, but the principal is still at risk due to market volatility. There are two types of variable

---

9   https://www.investopedia.com/terms/f/fixedannuity.asp

annuities with all types of riders. The variable annuity[10] is the product that people think of when they say annuities have high fees. I will explain the two types of variable annuities; then I'll explain the types of riders.

The first type is a Class A variable annuity. This type of annuity has front-loaded fees that range from approximately 2% up to 7% out of the initial deposit. If you put $100,000 into a Class A with a 6% front-loaded fee, you'll start with an initial account of $94,000. On top of that, there are all sorts of fees each year on the contract that range from approximately 2% to 4%.

The other type is a Class B variable annuity. This type of annuity does not have any front-loaded fees, but it does have annual fees of approximately 2% to 5% per year. This type of variable annuity has a surrender time frame just like the fixed annuity. The principal is also subject to market volatility.

Variable annuities all have prospectuses, and they range from 70 pages to some being over 300 pages long. These have to be the most complicated products in the market today. They do have riders that protect the death benefit and the

10 https://www.forbes.com/sites/feeonlyplanner/2012/07/02/9-reasons-you-need-to-avoid-variable-annuities/#3a75eebe5f19

income value, but those come at a high cost. Before you even entertain the thought of buying a variable annuity, ask the following questions:

1. What is the exact name of the insurance carrier?
2. What is the exact name of the product?
3. What class is it? (i.e., Class A, B, etc.)?
4. How much premium am I depositing?
5. How much of my premium is left after fees or what is my starting balance after fees?
6. What are the exact names of the optional riders that are included on this product?
7. What are all of the itemized fees and commissions associated with this product and its riders? Fees that are not active, but declared, can be added during the contract and almost all fees can be increased up to a maximum amount. You should not only ask what the current fees are, but what the potential maximum fees are. It is important to know that fees are applied even when your account value is decreasing due to market losses and erode account value increases due to market gains.

   a. **Transaction fee** (Class "A" annuities, charged by carrier)?

b. **Policy fee or Contract Maintenance fee** (Charged by carrier)?

c. **Broker fee** (Commission charged by the broker)?

d. **Mortality and Expense fee** (Fee to pay account balance as a death benefit, charged by the carrier)?

e. **Income Rider fee** (Fee to provide income on account balance or step-up amount, charged by the carrier)?

f. **Death Benefit Rider fee** (Fee to provide a step-up on the death benefit, charged by the carrier)?

g. **Fund Fees** (Charged by the Sub-Accounts)

   i. **Investment management fees** (Usually not disclosed or declared in the prospectus. This fee is usually never seen but reduces the return of your sub-accounts)?

   ii. **12b-1 fees** itemized for each recommended fund (Used to pay advertising expenses associated with the sub-accounts)?

   iii. **Fund Transfer fees** (This fee is paid when you move money from one sub-account to another)?

h. **Early Withdrawal fees** (Other than Class "A" annuities. A fee paid to withdraw your money from the annuity during the early withdrawal period, charged by the carrier)?

   i. What are the fee maximums for each fee (most fees can be increased during the contract up to a maximum)?

   j. Any other fees (Every insurance carrier uses different names for their fees, and some carriers have fees that are not common. Some fees may not be active but can be added during the contract)?

8. What percentage is the guaranteed step-up (annual guaranteed interest rate) for the income and/or death benefit, if any?

   a. Can I walk away with the guaranteed step-up or can it only be taken as income or as a death benefit?

   b. Does taking income require annuitization (the process of converting your account to income through annuitization cannot be reversed)?

   c. Is the guaranteed step-up compounded?

   d. Do I lose my step-up if I take withdrawals from my account value?

   e. What investments am I limited to as a result of having your recommended step-up rider?

9. Can I lose my principal due to market loss?

The biggest problem with the variable annuity is the cost of the fees. Each rider and fund has a fee attached to it. On top of that, there is no principal protection. As I said earlier, I believe these products are a wolf in sheep's clothing. Anytime I have a client pull out the prospectus of their variable annuity, they get upset when they realize the fees they're paying. I must say, there is no reason to get a product like this when you discover the details and benefits of the next annuity.

THE FIXED INDEXED ANNUITY

The Fixed Indexed Annuity[11] offers the best of both worlds. It has the safety of the fixed annuity with an opportunity to participate in some of the market gains. These products can offer 5% to 10% upfront bonuses and have income interest guarantees that range from 5% to 10% compounded or simple interest each year to be used for a guaranteed lifetime of income.

These contracts can be as short as three years and as long as sixteen years. Most of these will allow 10% free withdrawals from the index value per year. It is very important to know

---

11   https://www.annuityfyi.com/fixed-indexed-annuities/what-is-fixed-indexed/

though, that these products do have surrender fees if you go over the 10% free withdrawal. They can be very high, and you could lose a significant portion of the bonus. This should be used only as a retirement vehicle or Safe Money fund. This is not to be used for emergency money or money for which you need to get more than 10% per year during the contract period.

Here is an example of a chart depicting how the indexed gains from a couple of insurance companies compared to the Standard and Poor's in the last nineteen years. This is an example of how the Fixed Indexed Annuity would work if you pulled your funds from October of 1998 until now.

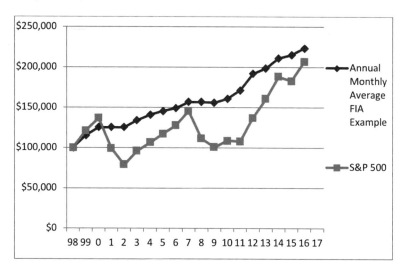

You can see from the chart that using the steady growth of the indexing provides a more secure way to use Safe Money strategies to protect your retirement and get a lifetime of risk-free money from the market. Risk Money always makes your retirement a guessing game leaving it up to chance. You see, with retirement accounts it's not about how high your account was, it's about what your retirement account value is when you retire.

The Fixed Indexed Annuity uses a fixed option as well as indexing options to determine the growth each year. Some use the S&P, DOW, Nasdaq, Hang Seng, Nikkei and some others. These are all different types of strategies. They can be one year, two years or longer point-to-point compounding growth.

With a Fixed Indexed Annuity, you do not get all the gains of the market, but you get none of the losses or risk of the market. The insurance company determines the gains based on the components called a cap, spread or a participation rate. Here are the definitions of each:

CAP RATE OR CAP

Some annuities may put an upper limit, or cap, on the index-linked interest rate. This is the maximum rate of interest the annuity will earn. If the index makes 10% and there is a 6% cap, you will get 6%. Not all annuities have a cap rate.

SPREAD/ADMINISTRATIVE FEE

In some annuities, the index-linked interest rate is computed by subtracting a specific percentage from any calculated change in the index. This percentage, sometimes referred to as the "margin," "spread," or "administrative fee," might be instead of, or in addition to, a participation rate. For example, if the calculated change in the index is 10%, your annuity might specify that 3% will be subtracted from the rate to determine the interest rate credited. In this example, the rate would be 7% (10% - 3% = 7%). In this example, the company subtracts the percentage only if the change in the index produces a positive interest rate.

PARTICIPATION RATE

The participation rate determines how much of the increase in the index will be used to calculate index-linked interest. For example, if the calculated change in the index is 10% and the participation rate is 70%, the index-linked interest rate for your annuity will be 7% (10% of 70% = 7%). A company may set a different participation rate for newly issued annuities as often as each day. Therefore, the initial participation rate in your annuity will depend on when the company issues it. The company usually guarantees the participation rate for a specific period (from one year to the entire term). When that period is over, the company sets a new participation rate for the next period. Some annuities guarantee that the participation rate will never be set lower than a specified minimum or higher than a specified maximum. Here is something a little more visual:

Market Gain	10%	10%	10%
	Cap 7%	Spread 3%	Participation rate 50%
Your Gain	7%	7%	5%

The Fixed Indexed Annuity is the only Safe Money product that can give you an upfront bonus, guaranteed income interest, protection of principal from market risk and income you can never outlive. It is my opinion that nothing compares to this product for a secure retirement and a lifetime of income.

QUESTIONS TO ASK YOURSELF:

➢ Which annuity is the best to protect my retirement principal and retirement income?

_____

_____

_____

➢ Does it make sense to take less of the market gains if I do not have to take any of the market loss?

_____

_____

_____

➢ What is my risk tolerance with my retirement money?

_____

_____

_____

Why Insurance Companies and Fixed or Fixed Indexed Annuities for Safe Money?

We have seen large financial institutions fail over the past decade, losing billions and billions of dollars and costing us taxpayers trillions in bailout money. The financial meltdown[12] has affected almost everyone in this country.

The banking industry has not been immune from failure. From 2009–2014, more than 500 banks failed. With potential market issues in the future, banks could continue to

___

12 https://www.thebalance.com/2008-financial-crisis-3305679

have major financial issues and even closures. Even as I write this book, banks are already starting to go back to doing loans and approving applicants in the same manner that got them into trouble in the first place.

How can our core institutions fail? How could banks ever have been allowed to be in such a situation? If the banking industry is so volatile, then how can we even trust them? The answer is simple. The banking industry in our country is safe and secure due to long-term legislation which guarantees our money to be safe.

The Federal Deposit Insurance Corporation (FDIC) backs deposits in its member banks up to $250,000. (See link for additional details: www.fdic.org). This guarantee provides safety and stability to the banking industry.

While the banking industry is regulated from the federal level, actual regulation is delegated to each state. The state regulators acting as the head of the spear examine the banks, their loan-to-asset ratios and their ability to serve their community. When an issue arises, the transparency to the federal regulators is instant. Safety and security in our banking industry are paramount to the success of our economy.

With Bear Sterns and other large financial firms closing, and financial scams and dishonest financial advisors and brokers the norm these days, people who just want to protect their nest egg are running in circles or paralyzed in fear. I have met with hundreds of clients, some of them crying because they don't know what to do and are scared to move anything.

It is time to look back to old faithful. For centuries, insurance companies have been some of the most stable institutions in the world. Insurance companies protect their money in unique ways that ensure safety for the insurance company and the people who place their money with them. How is it regulated and how safe is it? Other than a few hybrid companies, such as AIG, the insurance industry is well beyond fiscal repute. The insurance industry is regulated at the state level, and states communicate amongst themselves via the individual State Department of Insurance.

Insurance companies are also rated by third-party organizations that rate the insurance companies based on financial stability and reserves of the insurance company. Some of the main rating companies are A.M. Best, Standard and Poor's, and Moody's.

One hundred years ago, these organizations put into place underlying guarantees to make sure that insurance companies comply with state laws, fiscal responsibility, and fairness. To ensure the insurance companies performance, the inter-state State Guarantee Association was formed (http://www.ncigf.org).

Insurance companies are some of the most regulated of any financial institution. Combined with the underlying state guarantee fund, you'll discover incredible safety and peace of mind.

BOTTOM LINE:
WHY DO I WANT A FIXED INDEXED ANNUITY?

1. Protection of my principal and gains!
2. I do not have to worry about market ups and downs.
3. I am not losing sleep worrying about outliving my retirement.
4. I can participate in some of the market upswings but none of the downside.
5. I can pass the account value directly to my beneficiary.

6. I can get an income for the rest of my life.
7. I do not have to pay high broker fees.
8. My money will grow tax-deferred.
9. Liquidity. I can draw up to 10% per year.
10. SAFETY, SAFETY, SAFETY!

Without question, safety is a top priority for every person when they are saving their money. But safety means different things to different people. To some people, safety means putting money in the bank because banks have FDIC insurance.

To others, it means having money diversified across a variety of stocks. To some people, safety means picking their stocks after they have researched the underlying companies; and to others, it means entrusting their money to professionals.

I think we can agree that no one puts their money in a place where they expect to lose it. They put their money in a place where they expect to get it back one day; hopefully, after experiencing some nice growth. The great thing about fixed annuities is that they uniquely offer three levels of protection, which makes them the gold standard of safety.

Level No. 1: By contract, a fixed annuity guarantees that your principal is protected and that you can get it back again. There may be a penalty for early withdrawal, but as the annuity owner, you can control your withdrawals. So, no circumstance can cause you to lose money in a fixed annuity due to market volatility.

Level No. 2: Insurance companies rarely fail because they are heavily regulated by your state's Department of Insurance. State regulations require that insurance companies keep reserves (money held in safe investments like T-bills) to back up your policy value. Certain state programs also may provide an additional layer of protection (contact your department of insurance for further details).

Level No. 3: If you have a problem with the insurance company that issued your annuity and you want to get a regulator involved, the regulator is located in your home state no matter where that insurance company is located.

With these three levels of protection, there is nowhere with the same benefits that are safer for your money than a fixed annuity.

QUESTIONS TO ASK YOURSELF:

➢ Do I like the layers and history of safety and security Fixed Insurance companies offer?

_____

_____

_____

CHAPTER 12

Do You Have Money or Does Your Money Have You?

J ust as important as making sure your money is safe and
securing income for life, you also need to make sure you
are not consumed by debt. It is imperative to get rid of
your debt before you retire and get your monthly expenses
as low as possible. You cannot enjoy your retirement if you
are continually cash-strapped and barely making it month to
month.

I meet with retirees all the time who insist on living the
way they were accustomed to when they were working, even
though once they retired, their income was cut in half and

their debt remained the same, which kept their monthly expenses very high. I've also met with people who prepared well ahead of time, had very little to no debt, were able to save up enough for their retirement, and would not have to take a cut in their income. Which one would you want to be?

To accomplish this, one of the best things you could do is when you are about ten years from your retirement, stop buying anything on credit. If you don't have the cash to pay for it, you don't buy it. That cash needs to be on top of your savings and retirement. This concept is hard for a lot of people to follow! Nowadays, people rarely prepare for the future. It has been said that only 10% of people who retire are debt free. I love it when I sit across a table from someone, I'm gathering their financial information, and I find out they have prepared well for their retirement. I always smile and say, "You have done a great job, and now you should be able to truly enjoy your retirement."

All people, no matter what their age, should have a budget and be telling their money what to do and where to go. I run across people who spend $50 to $200 a week on frivolous things like coffee and sodas from the convenience store or grab a little bite to eat here and there but don't think twice about what they should put away for the future. They're like a little kid yelling mine, mine, mine, or I want this or I want that, throwing a fit if they don't get it. I have worked with youth for a little over a decade, and I have found that the young people of this generation have a strong entitlement attitude. They want what everybody else has, but are not willing to go through what it takes to get it.

Something given to you for free is rarely as appreciated as something you had to earn and work hard for. When I was in high school, I struggled to get good grades, no matter what my parents said or how many times I got grounded. It was amazing though, as soon as I had to pay for my own college, I turned into a straight-A student. My parents' jaws dropped when they saw my transcript and asked, "What happened?" I said, "I had to pay for it."

When you save and work hard to prepare for your retirement, you seem to enjoy it more and not take it for granted. That is also why so many seniors are heartbroken though, too. When you save for your retirement for so long and it's lost in the market because of lack of management from your broker, or the pension you've been told you would have is taken away, it makes you angry. It is time for people to tell their money what to do and secure a lifetime of income. If you do not tell your money what to do now, it will tell you what to do in the future.

QUESTIONS TO ASK YOURSELF:

➤ Do I have debt? Am I working to eliminate it?

_____

_____

_____

➤ Do I have a budget? Do I stick to it?

_____

_____

_____

➤ Do I spend frivolously?

_____

_____

_____

Do You Think You're an "A" List, Whale, Big Fish, Top-Tier Client to Your Advisor with the Amount of Funds You Have with Them Now?

O ver the years, I have found many disturbing articles, printouts, instruction letters, YouTube videos advising brokers, variable agents, and money managers to prioritize calls to their clients based on the amount of money someone has with them.

Here are some of the most disturbing things I have heard over the years on what these so-called "brokers, advisors, money managers" have been advised on how to prioritize their calls. They call their "A" list, Whale, Big Fish, Top-Tier

Clients (important people) first when the market drops or is unstable and don't worry about their little fish or bottom feeders (unimportant people), placing them at the bottom of their call list.

- Call your "A-List" clients first to let them know you are aware of the market volatility and are watching their accounts closely, to maintain your relationship with them.
- If a client does not have $500,000 or more to invest, then don't bother calling them, they are a waste of your time.
- Call the Big Fish first; they will cause the biggest ripples if you upset them.
- Maintain your Top-Tier clients first because most of your income depends on them.

I find this disturbing! Over the many years, I have been helping thousands of clients retire, I have found one thing to be true: the smaller the amount of money someone has, the greater the impact a big loss is to them.

Example: If you have $10,000,000 and you lose 50%, you still have $5,000,000. If you have $300,000 and you lose

50%, you only have $150,000 left. This is huge and makes it even worse if you are trying to draw an income for life.

Here are some other things I have heard about who they should help and how they should treat clients.

- Pick your top list of clients and invite them to special events you put on.
- Never spend too much time on a client with less than $500,000 to invest.
- When they have less money to manage, charge them a higher fee.
- We will only help clients with $500,000 or more to invest.

SEVEN QUESTIONS TO ASK YOURSELF ABOUT YOUR BROKER, BANKER, FINANCIAL PLANNER:

(Even though you ask these questions, I know they will only give you the answer they think you will want to hear.)

1. How far down the call list am I?

   _____

   _____

2. Will they even get to me in time before I lose a bunch of money in a market decline?

_____

_____

3. Why would someone base my value or importance on the amount of money I have with them?

_____

_____

4. If losing 10, 20, 30, 40, 50% of my money is a huge deal to me, why would it not be important to them?

_____

_____

5. Do I get charged a higher fee because I have less money to invest?

_____

_____

6. Do I have fewer investment options because I do not have a hefty sum of money to invest?

_____

_____

7. Do I want to risk my money in the market even if I am important to them?

Do not let anyone assume your value based on your net worth. It is a slap in the face for anyone to do this. Your money is important to you, so it should be important to anyone who is helping you with your Safe Money and Lifetime Income.

QUESTIONS TO ASK YOURSELF:

➤ Do I really think my broker will call me first when the market collapses, or will they attend to someone who has more money?

_____

_____

_____

➤ Do I like it that they will assume my value based on how much money I have with them?

_____

_____

_____

➤ Do they really manage my smaller accounts or are they put on autopilot trading by a computer?

_____

_____

_____

➤ Have they warned me at the top of the market, advising me to protect my gains or do they have the "let it ride" mentality, so I don't waste their time?

_____

_____

_____

How Do You Pick the Right Agent to Help You?

Currently, there are well over 1,200,000 life insurance agents[13] in the United States. How can you ever decide which one is best for you? On top of that, there's all this "fiduciary" stuff being thrown around to confuse you even more. Let me make something clear. If you are currently a life-licensed agent and you sell anything other than fixed products, you must be a fiduciary. So now that that's out of the way, let me give you some secrets on how to find out if the agent is as good as they say. For years, I've been

---

13 https://www.statista.com/statistics/194232/number-of-us-insurance-brokers-and-service-employees/

named by multiple organizations as one of the top 100 solo agents in the United States, so I am an expert in my field. There are a lot of expert imposters out there that I want to expose.

I know I'll ruffle some agents' feathers, but that has never stopped me before. My goal with this book is to help you, not them. I own another company that helps agents to represent these products honestly and ethically. Here are some tips to help you pick the right agent and listen for things they might say.

1. **I have access to all insurance companies.**
    a. This is usually a true statement. That being said, there is a big difference between having access to all companies and knowing which company has the best product for your situation.
    b. Make sure they show you at least ten other companies they have compared to see how and why they picked the best one for you.
2. **Make sure they leave you the State Insurance Buyers Guide.**
    c. If they don't leave this with you without being asked, that's a huge red flag. Each state insurance

commissioner has a buyer's guide that if you even mention the word annuity, you should receive.

3. **Make sure they leave you a copy of the illustration with ALL pages!**

   d. Agents can be lazy and not want to take the time to do this. YOU do not want a lazy agent!

   e. If they don't leave you an illustration with all the pages, how do you have proof of what they're telling you and how the product works?

4. **Make sure they leave you the Insurance Company product brochures.**

   f. Companies heavily suggest that the agent leaves all product materials with the client so they can do their own due diligence and research.

   g. Once again, how do you know if what they are telling is true if they don't leave the brochures from the insurance company which explain how the product works?

5. **Make sure all the illustrations are done by the company they are presenting and not on an Excel or Word spreadsheet.**

   h. No illustration is valid or accepted if it's not from their illustration software with the company information on it.

6. **Don't be impressed by a title or acronyms after their name.**

   i. So many agents have an extensive list of acronyms after their name that means nothing. There are so many web-based certifications that agents get sucked into that are not even recognized by the insurance industry.

   j. Knowledge, skillset, and expertise far surpass title.

7. **It does not matter how long they have been an agent.**

   k. Many times, the agents I have taught over the years have been slow to change to newer technology. Having the most up-to-date technology allows me to compare more companies to make sure I have the best product for them.

   l. Many agents barely get by year after year selling a few policies here and there. They have no business being in the insurance industry.

If you follow the recommended tips above, you should have a pretty good chance of picking the right financial person to help you with your retirement and income. If needed, take your time and make sure you do your own due diligence while making sure you have the right person helping you find the right financial products that solve any issues or concerns you might have.

QUESTIONS TO ASK YOURSELF:

➤ Is my agent showing me something that compares multiple companies?

_____

_____

_____

➤ Did they leave me the State Insurance Buyers Guide and all other company brochures and illustrations?

_____

_____

_____

➤ Have I done my own research?

_____

_____

_____

Final Thoughts – Sleep Insurance

T he goal for writing this book was to write it in English and not "financialese." I want people to understand how to get the best product for themselves and their retirement. Too many times, the financial world wants to talk over your head, wanting you to feel too stupid to ask any questions, hoping that you'll need them to translate the financial world for you. I want to empower you to make educated decisions based on what you feel comfortable doing, not what they are selling you to do!

People's retirements continue to rise and fall on the stormy waves of the market. Too many times, we choose to ignore the storm and hope for the best. We continue to get market amnesia, forgetting about the 50% we lost in the market two years or ten years ago, still hoping to recover the losses. It's easy not to place real value to numbers on paper. For example, say you get the statement from your broker, and you read it went from $100,000 to $50,000. It has far less impact than if you laid that $100,000 in cash in the middle of your table and your broker started throwing $50,000 into the fireplace. Would you stand there and watch your broker do that? Of course not! You would tackle them to the ground and throw them out of your house. Why is it when it's on paper, we simply watch it burn? On top of that, so many people continue to allow their broker to manage their money and continue to pay them high fees.[14]

You need to stop buying into false hope and take charge of protecting your retirement. You need to fireproof your retirement and put your money into guaranteed accounts.

---

14 https://www.investopedia.com/articles/personal-finance/112515/are-fees-depleting-your-retirement-savings.asp

Brokers will warn you not to put your money into fixed indexed annuities because of the high surrender fees. If a fixed indexed annuity has a surrender fee of 12% in the first year and continues to go down year after year but your broker or financial planner has lost you 50% in the market, which one has the higher surrender fee? It is important to look at the big picture and the ulterior motives of the risk money manager. The risk money manager does not want you to move your money away from them because the second you do, they stop getting their fees.

One day, I took my four kids sledding. They talked me into going up the hill and sledding down it. I fell off and landed hard after I flew off this jump we built. After a few more times, it took a little longer to get up. So, I finally decided just to watch my kids have fun. It made me think of something. When I was a teenager, I could sled off the biggest jumps, tumble down the hill, run back up the hill and be able to do that all day. Now as a father of four, I can only do it for an hour or so before I throw in the towel. My grandfather, no matter how much we tried to get him up that hill, would smile and say, "I'll just watch you kids have fun."

Likewise, before you make any decisions about your money, here is a list of questions you should ask yourself.

HOW DO I FEEL ABOUT MY MONEY AND THE CURRENT SITUATION I AM IN?

20 Things to Ask Myself About My Retirement and Income for Life:

1. Do I like losing money in the market?

   _____

   _____

2. How does it make me feel when I lose money in the market?

   _____

   _____

3. Do I want to get my money safe?

   _____

   _____

4. Do I like the idea of having money guaranteed for the rest of my life?

   _____

   _____

CHAPTER 15

5. Do I like the idea of never worrying about market volatility?

_____

_____

6. Does this make sense to me?

_____

_____

7. Do I like the idea of this?

_____

_____

8. Do I want to go ahead and move forward with this no market risk product?

_____

_____

9. If I pass away, how much of the pension does my spouse get?

_____

_____

10. Do I really want my spouse to worry about how to get by when I am not around?

_____

_____

11. Wouldn't I like to make sure that even if I'm not around, my spouse will have guaranteed income for the rest of her life?

_____

_____

12. Am I comfortable losing all my money, some of my money or none of my money?

_____

_____

13. Do I like the idea that my broker makes money even when I lose money?

_____

_____

14. How do I plan to afford LTC?

_____

_____

15. It can be said that the two most common killers of seniors are stress and rocking chairs. Stress because you worry about losing your retirement and rocking chairs because you have nothing to live for or no money to do anything. If I put my retirement with this type of

product, I could reduce those two killers greatly. Does it make sense to do this?

_____

_____

16. What type of insurance do I have for my retirement?

_____

_____

17. Do I think I can really recover from significant losses even when I am taking out money to live off and pay my broker's high fees?

_____

_____

18. Have I thought about the loss of the lower social security income if one of us passes away?

_____

_____

19. Do I have time to recover from another major market drop?

_____

_____

20. Do I lose sleep at night when I am losing large amounts of money in the market?

_____

_____

You see, we need to look at our retirement the same way. When we're young, we can afford to take some risk, but as we get older, we need to limit our risk, and toward retirement, we need to simply get out of risk. When we're younger, our bodies heal fast. But as we get older, it takes longer to heal and our bodies ache for a little longer. Retirement money is the same way! Risk is not an option for your retirement.

I hope this book has helped you understand and uncover the lies that are being told to you about "Risk Money" as I shared with you the truth about "Safe Money" accounts (Fixed and Fixed Indexed Annuities). The whole purpose of this book is to present to you a new type of insurance… Sleep Insurance. When you don't have to worry about your retirement, you sleep better at night, and you're able to avoid the two common killers of seniors, Stress and Rocking Chairs.

If you would like to comment on how this book has helped you, you need any more information, or you need to find a Safe Money advisor in your area, go to www.eagleshadowlifeandannuity.com.

Have a safe retirement and God Bless.

———～～———